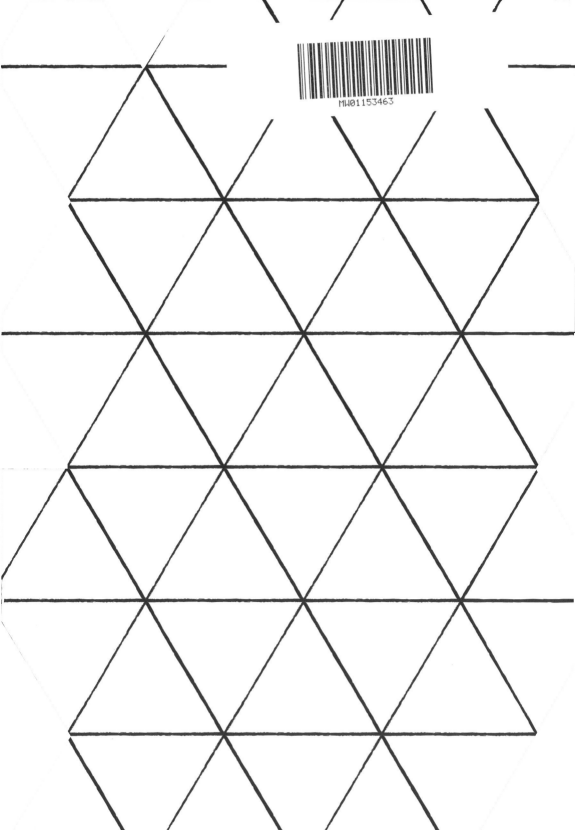

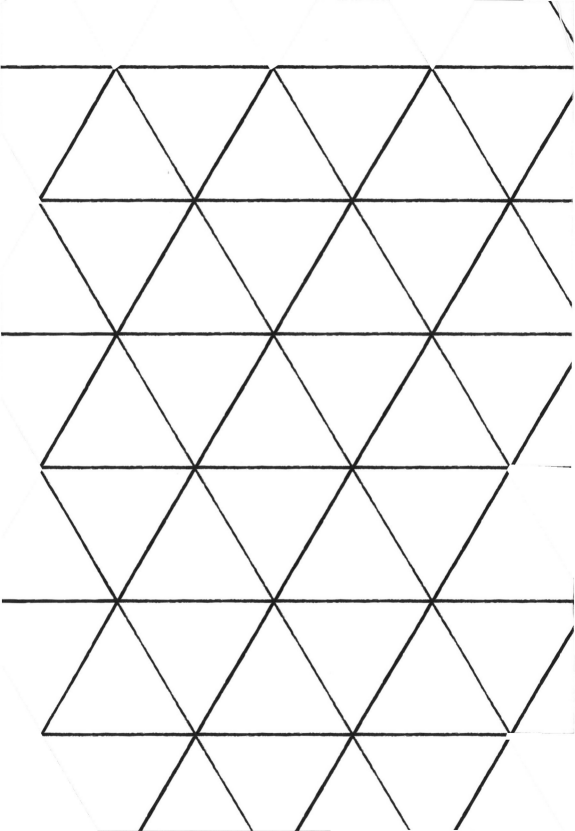

COLORAMA

COLORAMA

From Fuchsia to Midnight Blue

Cruschiform

Prestel

Munich • London • New York

For my parents

© for the original French edition: Gallimard Jeunesse, 2017
Gallimard Jeunesse Giboulées sous la direction de Colline Faure-Poirée et Hélène Quinquin
© for the English edition: Prestel Verlag, Munich • London • New York, 2017
A member of Verlagsgruppe Random House GmbH, Neumarkter Straße 28, 81673 Munich

◆

I
recall
the   at-
traction that
certain   colors
had on me when I
was a child: the red
poppy tails, both delicate
and strikingly powerful; the
green lichen that covered our
holiday home; the beige herds of
sheep migrating across the Cevennes
mountain range; the yellow, pungent
earth-working equipment that seemed to sing
to us; the violet stained beetroots; the black
licorice candy that my grandfather used to love
so much; the graying blue colors, understated and
hard to explain, that we once used to describe Mediterranean plants... Nowadays, I simply like a color for what
it is and for the memories it brings to me, as well as
the ideas and stories it conjures up. Ultimately,
each color has a history. Subjective and individual, singular and plural, this story is based
at the same time on our own perceptions.
The world of color is far more complex
than it seems. Perception of colors
fully depends on who we are,
our cultures and what era we
live in. It has to do with
sensibility and subjec-
tivity. There are no
two people who
see or de-scribe
a shade in
the same
way.

◆

WHITE **SNOW**

What would the winter be without its white cloak? Once the temperature drops below freezing, the air becomes so cold that the humidity in the clouds transforms itself into tiny little ice crystals. Depending on where the wind is swaying, these hexagonal, star-shaped crystals merge into flakes that then progressively coat the landscape. With this layer of striking whiteness, a moment of peace has arrived...

MILK

People have been drinking milk since the time when animals first became domesticated. That's about 12,000 years ago. This natural liquid, mainly produced by female mammals for their young, is mostly water. It owes its color to tiny milk proteins and globules of fatty matter. When these two substances combine, they can reflect light in a way that makes the milk liquid look white.

PEACE SYMBOL

According to the bible, God was disappointed with the world he had created. So he decided to conjure up an almighty deluge. He asked Noah to build him a sailing vessel to save every species of animal. Once the rain finally came to an end, Noah released a white dove to scout around. The bird later returned with an olive branch announcing the end of the divine wrath. That's how the white dove became an international peace symbol.

ALBINOS

Mice and rabbits aren't the only animals that can be albinos. Humans, mammals, birds, fish, amphibians, reptiles — all of these can be albinos, too! Extremely rare, they stand out from the crowd with their perfectly white color, their clear eyes and their pinkish irises. Albinos have an unusual change in their genes that affects their skin. Basically, they're missing a pigment called melanin, which gives normal skin its color.

ALABASTER

Alabaster is a limestone rock used to make small objects and sculptures since ancient times. Usually milky white and sometimes with honey-yellow streaks, this rock is more delicate than marble yet equally as precious.

Alabaster usually contains the mineral calcite or the mineral gypsum. Calcite alabaster was used by the ancient Egyptians, while gypsum alabaster was more common in Europe.

P☉LAR WHITE

Is it a coincidence that polar bears live in the snow-covered Arctic? Not at all.... According to the English naturalist Charles Darwin, this animal's coat has adapted itself to its environment. Its white fur acts as a perfect camouflage to help the bear survive. The animal's black skin contrasts with its fur and helps it conserve its body heat. Sadly though, this powerful creature is threatened by climate change through global warming.

COTTON FLOWER

People first grew cotton more than 3,000 years ago. After blossoming, cotton flowers change into cushioned pods of soft, white vegetable fiber. Then, when they burst open to release their seeds, the fiber is picked and turned into yarn and other woven materials, which can be used to create all types of fabrics. At present, cotton flower is the most worn textile in the world.

BIRCH BARK

The white birch tree primarily grows in North America and Russia. Like the poplar, it has adapted to harsh, cold climates. Its white bark with black speckles acts as a type of protective layer. Birch bark is also strongly reflective and therefore limits heat absorption and protects the tree against the winter frost. Simply put, white birch bark is the ultimate thermostat!

WHITE **MOTH**

During the early 1800s, industrial cities in England were swelling with people and factories. Soot from chimneys blackened city trees, and the white peppered moths who lived in these trees could no longer use their color to hide from predators. Over time, the insects adapted to their new environment by changing their color and becoming black peppered moths!

WHITE **POWDER**

During the time when France was ruled by kings, French aristocrats, both male and female, delighted in powdering themselves. This whitening was said to give them a genuine mark of distinction! However, in order to get a face whiter than white, the nobility started to use powders containing white lead. These powders may have been popular, but they were extremely toxic, too!

MARSHMALLOWS

Marshmallows are a sweet candy that the English like to toast when outdoors at a summer evening campfire. They take their name from the root extract of the marshmallow plant, which has an aromatic and succulent taste. In some countries, this root is also used as a chewing stick, especially for young children and their baby teeth!

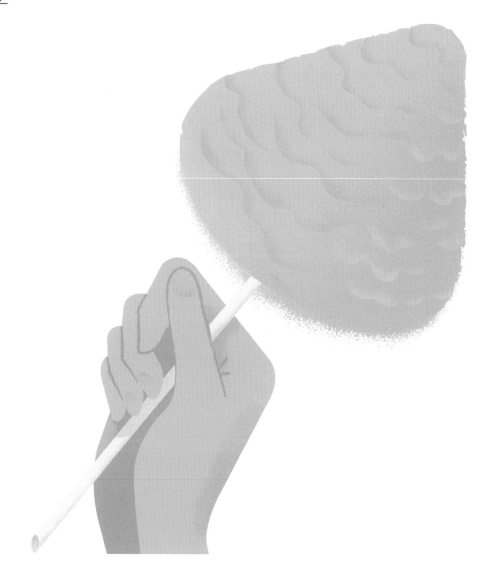

COTTON CANDY

How can anyone resist this confectionary treat? Nicknamed "candy floss" by the English and "fairy floss" by the Australians, its soft texture melts when placed below the tongue. Yet, cotton candy is made simply of pigments and sugar turned into a sweet yarn! It's very yummy, but not very good for our teeth. An American dentist invented it at the end of the nineteenth century. Maybe he knew it would keep people coming to his office?!

PINK **PIGGY**

Domesticated for its meat since Stone Age times, the pig is a descendant of the wild boar. Over the centuries, breeding and farming have given rise to many different types: some are more or less hairy and some more or less colorful. The great white, with its pink and silky skin, is a pig that took a long time to breed at the end of the nineteenth century. Today, however, it's become a staple of the farmyard.

BABY PINK

In Western countries today, soft pink is the color for girls' things, whereas pastel blue is the color for boys. Yet, this has not always been the case. It was quite opposite in the Middle Ages. Pink, an offshoot of the color red, was thought to represent the warrior and the soldier: the man. Blue was used to represent the Virgin Mary and all things feminine.

ROSE

The color rose does not owe its name to the pinkish rose flower, but to its ancestor, the rose hip. Both flowers are known for their fragrance and for their five delicate petals. In ancient times, the rose plant was said to have the power to ward off rabies from dogs. This is why it is sometimes referred to as "dog rose," or by its botanical name Rosa canina.

CHERRY BLOSSOM

There is no more beautiful sight in nature than a Sakura cherry tree in full blossom. In springtime, this tree is covered by a thick fleece of many little flowers that then scatter wherever the breeze takes them.

The Sakura is very popular in Japan, the Land of the Rising Sun. Here, its fleeting beauty is much associated with warriors, such as the famous Samurai swordsmen.

PINK

In the English language, pink is the name given to a wide variety of colors that are produced by lightening the color red. Pink refers to tenderness and love in most Western cultures. And in the English-speaking world, it often reminds us of the carnation. This flower was also known as the "flower of the gods," as it was used by the ancient Greeks to crown the heads of victorious athletes.

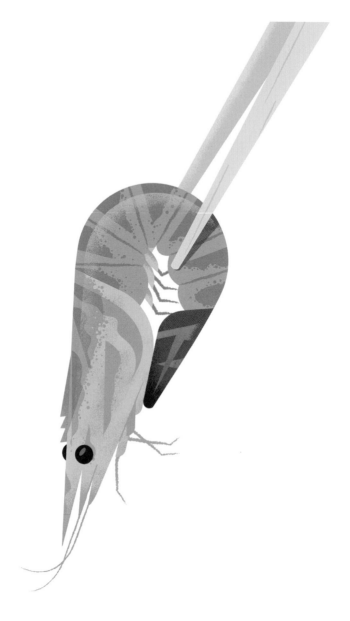

PINK **SHRIMP**

Shrimps live at the sandy bottom of the deep, where they feed on dead creatures. In this natural environment, the shrimp's carapace (or upper shell) is a translucent gray and offers the perfect camouflage.

Only when the animal is placed in a hot pan does its color turn pink. This change is due to astaxanthin, a natural pinkish-red pigment that is released within the shrimp's flesh at the moment it is cooked.

PINK **FLAMINGO**

Why are flamingoes pink? Surely it's down to their love of eating shrimp! Both owe their color to a pigment called astaxanthin, which exists in the algae of the marshes they inhabit. Flamingoes love to devour huge numbers of these tiny crustaceans, which makes their plumage turn progressively pink. Without the algae, both shrimp and flamingo would be white!

RISING SUN

Located off the eastern edge of Asia is Japan, a country nicknamed the Land of the Rising Sun. Its flag features a red circle that symbolizes the rising sun. For though we perceive the sun as yellow when high in the sky, we see it as reddish at the dawn and rise of each day. This change of color is due to the positions of the stars and how their light is dispersed through the atmosphere.

POMME GRENADE

Initially called a "pomme grenade," in reference to the dark red garnet gemstone, the pomegranate is a fruit containing up to 400 seeds that bursts when it becomes ripe. The old name for this "exploding" fruit was also used for a famous weapon — the military grenade. When the earliest types of grenades exploded, they released hundreds of deadly pellets... pellets that looked a lot like pomegranate seeds!

RED **KISSES**

Lipstick has been a weapon of seduction for thousands of years. Yet, it has always concealed less than lovely ingredients! In earlier times, it could be a mixture of crushed algae balm or blackberries; or maybe a blend of mashed cochineal insects and calf bone oil. Nowadays, people make lipstick with artificial colors and shark liver oil. Such beautiful materials to embellish your smile!

CANNONBALL RED

Where does this expression come from: "to see red"? Nowadays, it usually refers to someone suddenly becoming very angry. This turn of phrase has its roots, however, as far back as the seventeenth century, when soldiers used to heat their cannonballs in hot ovens until they became a blazing red. In short, they were not content with blasting away at the buildings of their enemies; they also wanted to burn them down!

RUBY

The deep red ruby and the intense blue sapphire are actually from the same family of minerals: the corundum. The ruby owes its color to the presence of chrome within its crystals. It is a precious, rare, expensive and favored stone in the world of jewelry. Rubies are notably found on the fingers of cardinals in the Roman Catholic Church, in order to complement their red cardinal habits (or tunics).

OXBLOOD

At the beginning of the twentieth century, Falu red (also known as oxblood) was widespread throughout the countryside of North America and Scandinavia. Used mainly to coat barns, this deep red pigment was made from ochre rock that was baked and then combined with linseed oil. The pigment not only looked nice, it also helped to repel insects. Rest assured, however, that real ox blood was never used to make the paint!

RED **PENNSY**

At the end of the nineteenth century, the powerful Pennsylvania Railway company laid 10,000 miles (16,000 kilometers) of track. Nicknamed Pennsy, the railway had an array of passenger trains that chiefly connected people between New York and Chicago. Its cars were decorated in a dark red paint containing wood from Brazil. Easy to make out in the landscape, these carriages became the trademark of the company.

027

CARMINE

Carmine (or crimson lake) is a natural, organic pigment that is produced by the female cochineal insect. Also known as the "scarlet seed," this tiny insect has been used by dye-makers over the centuries to produce a rich color for fabrics. Carmine has also been used as an ingredient to color food and cosmetics. Who would have foreseen such an unexpected role for this insect?

CARDINAL RED

A cardinal is a little bird that lives mainly in the United States, Canada and Mexico. It gets its name from the striking red plumage of the adult male. Cardinals of the Catholic Church wear clothes of a similar red color.

These high-ranking dignitaries did not choose the color by chance, as it is widely thought to symbolize power, excellence and love. The red shade also calls to mind the blood of Jesus Christ.

029

POPPY

What do the poppy and the crest of a rooster have in common? Surely, it is the color! But not only that... In old French, the name of this flower also refers to the rooster's song. In England, poppy flowers have become a symbol for veteran soldiers. Every spring they cloak the English fields in blood red — a reminder of the bloodshed sacrificed by soldiers in war.

ROOSTER

With his beautiful red crest, the rooster reigns supreme in the barnyard. Just listen to his mighty crow at the crack of every dawn: cocorico! That's how it is written in French. This song sounds a lot different in other countries, however... Germans hear kikeriki, English hear cock-a-doodle-doo and in Indonesia they understand kukuruyuk. Different cultures can perceive the same animal in different ways!

031

FERRARI® RED

The insignia of the famous Italian Ferrari® brand, this color can trace its origins back to the start of motor racing. At the beginning of the twentieth century, there began a great passion for this new mechanical sport.

Very quickly, particular colors were attributed to the vehicles of each country: blue for France, green for England, white for Germany and... red for Italy.

RED **CARD**

In some sports, especially football (or soccer), the referee may use different cards to interrupt the game and point out a violation made by a certain player. In reality, this has the same significance for the player as do traffic lights: yellow for caution and red for stop! In the case of soccer, when the referee shows a red card he is ejecting the player from the game.

033

ENGLISH RED

What would England be without its English red? From the eighteenth century, soldiers of the British army were dressed in a scarlet red tunic. This color may have been an aesthetic choice, but it was also a highly strategic one: during battle, the enemy found it difficult to discern the number of wounded. Nowadays, the color red is found on other famous British objects, such as buses and traditional phone boxes.

034

INDIAN SUMMER

An Indian summer is a prolonged period of warm weather that can last into the autumn. The leaves on the trees are transformed by delicate shades of red. This color is made by a pigment called anthocyanin, which occurs naturally in the leaves' cells. Hidden away throughout the summer by the green of another pigment called chlorophyll, anthocyanin spreads within the leaves as the chlorophyll fades away.

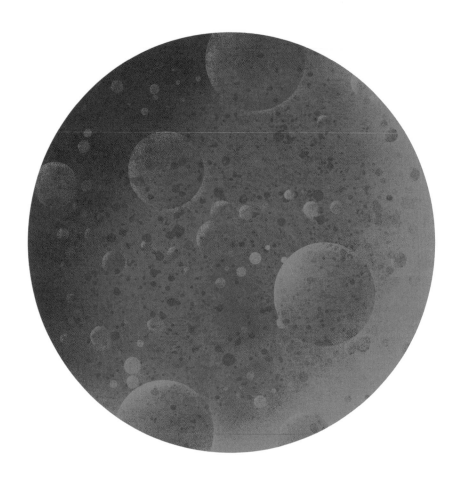

035

MARS RED

The planet Mars can be seen from Earth with the naked eye! The ancient Romans greatly admired this planet, and they named it after their god of war. Mars owes its shade to a metal compound called ferric oxide, which is contained in the rocks that cover its surface. The Earth also has these kinds of reddish rocks, where corrosion has taken place and produced rust.

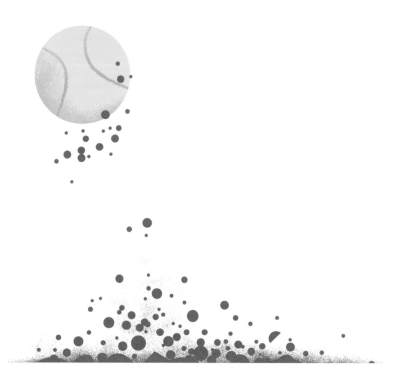

036

CLAY

In the late 1800s, two English brothers named Renshaw were on vacation in Cannes, when they decided to organize a tennis club there. After first building grass-covered courts, they soon noticed their grass could not tolerate the Mediterranean climate. They therefore covered the courts with a powder they had created by baking recycled earthenware clay pots. The first clay courts had been invented!

037

SAFFRON

Saffron (or "red gold") is a spice obtained by drying out crocus flowers. The spice has been cultivated for thousands of years. It is mostly found nowadays in the Middle East. Known to be the most expensive spice in the world, its delicacy and fragility justify its price. Moreover, harvesting takes place over a short period, and it's still done by hand!

ORANGE

Around 1500, Portuguese explorers in China tasted a fruit they'd never seen before: the orange. They brought the fruit back with them in their luggage, and it soon became a luxury item in Europe! Today, it is one of the most popular foods in the world. Its peel and its flesh are filled with a pigment called anthocyanin, which due to the fruit's acidity turns orange. Other fruits also contain anthocyanin, but they often turn red.

039

CARROT

The carrot plant is cultivated in all temperate regions of the world, and it's only grown for its root. Whilst the most known variety is orange in color, carrots can also come in red, purple, yellow or even white. It all depends on its species and its content of... carotene! This natural orange pigment is also responsible for coloring melons, sweet potatoes and pumpkins. But it does not occur in the orange fruit!

CARROT TOP

The expression "carrot top" is used to describe a person with red hair. It comes from the title of a novel by French author Jules Renard. The novel depicts the tough childhood of a redhead. This golden tinged color occurs when there is a higher concentration of pheomelanin pigment in the hair. Redheads are rare — they do not even represent more than 2-3% of the world's population. And the place you find them most is Scotland!

041

FAWN

The French word "fauve" and the English word "fawn" derive from the German word "falwa," meaning an animal or object that is "yellow bordering on red." Today, the English word usually refers to the color itself or to a young deer. But in France, "fauve" has come to describe lions, tigers, cheetahs, and other wild cats at the top of the food chain.

AMBER

Millions of years ago, resin dripped off the pine trees of the Baltic region in Europe. This simple tree sap fossilized over time to form the beautiful, gem-like material called amber, with its multiple shades of yellow.

Amber is especially significant if it contains small insects or microscopic creatures from the faraway era when it was formed.

043

CAMEL HAIR

It's not just sheep, goat or llama hair that can be turned into wool. Camel hair is good for this purpose as well! For many centuries, the people of Mongolia and Kazakhstan bred camels for their fleece, which they used to make clothing and carpets. This so-called "camel hair" is a thick textile with a dark ochre color. Although camel hair is mostly left in its natural color, the fleece can be dyed in the same way as wool fibers.

044

OCHRE

Ochre encompasses a wide variety of pigments made from rocks and clay, ranging in color from red and brown to yellow. One of the most famous types of ochre comes from the region around Sienna, in central Italy.

Originating from the Paleolithic period, it was highly appreciated by prehistoric people called the Cro-Magnon. They ground the clay into a powder and then used it to make paintings and frescoes on cave walls.

045

KHAKI

In Persian, khaki actually means "soil" or "dust." We tend to associate the color with camouflage or hunting. It was the British army in the nineteenth century that first adopted the shade to clothe its troops. In earlier centuries, soldiers wore vibrant colors to better distinguish themselves from ordinary people. But modern soldiers wear clothes that help them blend into their natural surroundings and escape the enemy.

046

OFF-WHITE

Off-white or gray refers to the color of silk in its raw form. We owe this precious material to the Bombyx mori, or "silkworm" as it is better known. This caterpillar secretes a thread that it uses for its cocoon, the cocoon from which it emerges as a moth. Silkworms can produce thread as long as 5,000 feet (1,500 meters), but it's up to people to transform it into the luxurious material we all know as silk.

BEIGE

Initially, the word beige referred to the wooly coats of sheep and certain other animals. These animals are shorn every spring. First, their hair is sorted, washed, combed and spun into balls that will later be knitted.

Farming wool dates back to the beginning of humankind. Moreover, depending on the human culture, different types of beige appear as goat cashmere, Angora rabbit and camel hair...

048

EGG SHELL

As a color, "egg shell" refers specifically to the fresh eggs of farm-reared red hens. In France they are usually beige, and in America they are white. If all birds laid eggs with a hue that corresponded to their color, size and shape, then there would even be blue eggs, too. Have you ever wondered how birds' bodies make this protective wrapper around their eggs? By using the pebbles that the birds eat, of course!

049

DESERT ROSE

Despite its name, the desert rose is not a plant. It is actually a rock crystal that forms when materials in desert sand evaporate and crystallize. This phenomenon takes place over thousands of years, and it occurs mainly in soft and sandy terrain from hot regions where the nights are humid. The crystals fuse into strips and take on the appearance of rose petals.

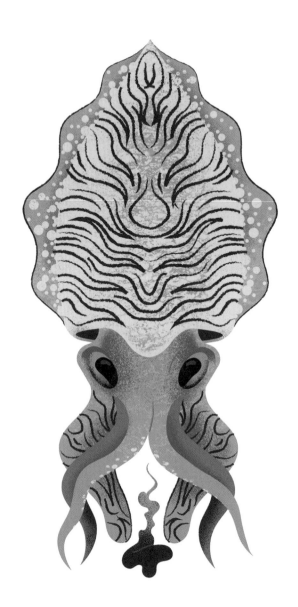

050

SEPIA

What do photography and mollusks have in common? The answer is sepia! Also known as cuttlefish ink, this liquid is discharged by cuttlefish, octopus, squid and other kinds of sea mollusks. The ink is squirted into the eyes of predators that get too close, enabling the mollusks to escape and go into hiding. It is also a colorant used in cooking and graphic arts... It is even the name given to a photographic print.

051

TURMERIC

Much appreciated by food connoisseurs, turmeric is a highly fragranced spice in many Asian cultures. Nicknamed "terra merita" in Latin, it was meant to signify both an earthy substance and human virtues. The yellow powder from the rhizome (or underground stem) of the turmeric plant is used as a seasoning, a cosmetic, a health treatment and a dye. Buddhist monks also use turmeric to color their costumes.

052

INDIAN YELLOW

Indian yellow is a vivid and bright color in sunlight. As early as the fifteenth century it was being used in Indian art. Legend tells that the pigment was produced from the urine of cows that had been fed only mango leaves and water. Once the water evaporated, the urine formed a paste that was then reduced into a powder and then a pigment. Sadly, the cows would die a couple years later because of this terrible treatment!

053

CATERPILLAR®

Caterpillar® is a company known through-out the world for its construction equip-ment — bulldozers, shovel loaders, excavators, etc. Founded in the United States, the firm owes its name to its tractors, which were thought to crawl like caterpillars. These imposing vehicles still catch people's eyes with their bright yellow paintwork. Yellow is also a signal that people — especially con-struction workers — are on the job.

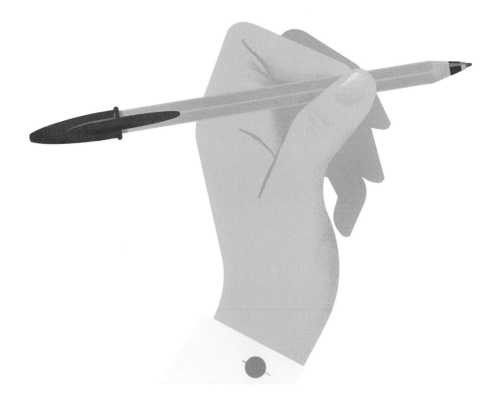

054

BIC®

The French company BIC® is the world's largest manufacturer of ballpoint pens. It was named after the founder, Marcel Bich, who revolutionized writing habits when he acquired the patent for pens in the 1950s and launched the BIC in a characteristic orange shade. László József Bíró had already invented the pen in 1938 in Hungary. Even today, this iconic writing utensil is found in school backpacks worldwide.

055

EGG YOLK

The yolk of an egg is an indispensable source of nutrition for the bird embryo in its shell. Rich in lipids (or fats), it owes its color to lutein, which is a colored pigment found in many foodstuffs and plants. Some might think that lutein is responsible for the color of the down in chicks. In fact, the birds' genes determine the hue, which is why we find chicks in all colors: from yellow, brown and black to speckled ones.

056

SECURITY YELLOW

If the color red stands for "danger" or "stop" on street signs, then it is yellow that universally serves as a warning color. Yellow grabs your attention. Easily recognizable from a distance, especially when it's dawn or dusk, yellow was overwhelmingly adopted as the color for American school buses in order to guarantee the safety of American school kids.

SUNFLOWER

In the plant world, flowers have bright colors in order to attract the attention of foraging insects. The petals of the sunflower are a flamboyant yellow. Its flexible, pale purple stalk enables the plant to tilt toward the sun throughout the whole day. Characteristic of southern France, sunflowers became immortalized in paintings by Vincent van Gogh, who was truly passionate about the vibrancy of their colors!

058

PØLLEN

When it comes to the cultivation of plants, pollen is an absolute necessity. Pollen helps make it possible for plants to bear fruit, and bees are often the animals that transport pollen from one plant to another. Bees also harvest nectar from the flowers to make their chief source of food: honey. To produce about one pound (500 grams) of honey, the bees would need to make about 50,000 trips.

059

CANARY YELLOW

Canary yellow is named after a little bird known for its yellow plumage and its beautiful song: the canary bird from the Canary Islands. In order to intensify their plumage, some canary breeders feed the birds with lutein-rich foods, such as rape, colze and related seeds. This is also done in chicken breeding so that lutein can tint the birds' flesh.

IVORY

For many centuries, ivory has been used to make a whole range of precious items: billiard balls, white piano keys and shirt buttons. This material is extracted from the tusks of certain animals that, unfortunately, are becoming endangered: elephants, hippopotamuses, walruses, warthogs, etc. These days, such species are protected, and people have turned to plastic as an ivory substitute.

061

FLOWERS OF SULPHUR

This bright yellow material has been prized since ancient times, when people used it in thermal baths to treat certain illnesses. Flowers of sulphur is made from grinding down natural sulphur, a material that often forms around active volcanoes. In seventeenth-century Italy, this same pigment was collected at Mount Vesuvius and sold to artists. It later became known as the "Yellow of Naples."

GLOWWORM

What a pleasure it is to see a worm shining on a summer's night! In fact, the glowworm is something like a caterpillar — a creature that matures into a winged insect. Glowworms and fireflies are both part of the same family of insects. As night falls, they emit a yellowish-green light from their abdomen. This light is produced through a process called bioluminescence.

063

KIWI GREEN

Let us head off to New Zealand and discover the kiwi fruit. The term kiwi actually refers to both a fruit and an animal, which is no coincidence! The berry-shaped kiwi fruit has green and sweet flesh, and its name comes from the Maori people. These native New Zealanders named it after their country's famous kiwi bird, because the fruit's skin is hairy and resembles the bird's gray-brown plumage.

064

BEDBUG

Widespread in Europe, this green bug often hides in gardens, leafy forests and wetlands. Is it harmless? Not a chance... Whenever the insect feels threatened, it emits a sickening odor that can drive away its enemy.

Nevertheless, it is still a bit of a show-off. As winter approaches it dresses in brown, and for the return of springtime it is green — always customizing itself to its environment.

065

GREEN **WITH ANGER**

Why do we use the expression "green with anger"? The word "anger" originates from the Latin term "cholera," which actually means "excess of bile." Bile is a greenish fluid that is discharged by our gallbladder for digesting food. But when people developed certain gallbladder diseases, the complexion of their skin could turn greenish. These people are a bit like the Hulk, who also turns green when he becomes discontented!

066

CHLOROPHYLL

The main pigment responsible for the green color of plants is chlorophyll. This pigment also enables plants to grow. Chlorophyll uses sunlight energy and converts it in a process called photosynthesis. In exchange, trees and plants discard oxygen that is essential to our survival. This is why we got the idea of naming our great forests "the lungs of the earth."

B**O**TTLE GREEN

Why is wine kept in green bottles? Red wine is extremely sensitive to light. In order to protect it from sunlight and to preserve its taste, colored bottles are used. Each bottle's color, ranging from brown to dark green, depends on the amount of iron oxide used in its manufacture. Wine bottles often give the illusion that the liquid contained inside is actually black.

068

BRITISH GREEN

Just like Ferrari® red, British green (or racing green) has its origins in the history of motor racing. At the beginning of the twentieth century, each country adopted a color so that they would stand out on the racing track: blue for France, white for Germany, red for Italy and, with a dark green shade and many victories, the English and their very British green.

CEDAR BLUE

A majestic tree from the conifer family, the blue cedar is instantly recognizable by its blue-gray needles. Originally from North Africa, this tree is capable of growing up to 130 feet (40 meters) high and living more than 900 years. The cedar blue is now the national symbol of Lebanon, and it can be admired on that country's snowy peaks. It is also considered a sacred tree, associated with eternity and peace.

070

LINCOLN GREEN

In the thirteenth century, the small town of Lincoln, located close to Sherwood Forest in England, had gained a reputation for making fabrics. What was its specialty? It is said they used green materials! This may be why Robin Hood, archer to the Earl of Lincoln and an intrepid outlaw, is described in so many traditional folk tales as dressed in green whilst robbing from the rich and giving to the poor.

071

ARSENIC

By the beginning of the twentieth century, Paris was infested by rats. In order to exterminate them, an arsenic-based poison was developed: the green of Paris. This horribly toxic powder was also used as a pigment by painters of that day, in spite of the risks it presented. Thus, it could be said that Cezanne, Monet and even van Gogh were progressively poisoning themselves whilst making their colorful art.

072

GLAUCOUS

This word refers to subtle colors that combine dull blue, green and gray. Discovered in the leaves of Mediterranean plants such as lavender, sage and artichoke, these tones help the plants survive in their challenging environment. The plants' leaves are covered in a glaucous-colored substance to protect them from the arid climate and strong sunshine... a natural sunblock!

LICHEN

Lichen is a small organism, something that looks halfway between fungus and seaweed. Some varieties can withstand extreme climates: intense dryness, glacial frosts, etc. In the case of reindeer lichen, a plant of the Arctic, it serves as a vital food for wild reindeer herds during the long winter months. Thus, it is the first link in a fragile ecosystem.

074

CELADON

This delicate shade of green and blue is much cherished in Asia because of its similarity to a sacred stone called jade. Korean ceramic makers developed the chemical process for making Celadon hundreds of years ago. In this process, colored enamel is applied on pieces of clay, which are then baked at over 1,800 degrees Fahrenheit (1,000 degrees Celsius).

VERDIGRIS

This word meaning green-gray derives from the old French term "vertegrez," which is used to describe any colored object that has become "green produced by acid." In reality, the process of making verdigris involves a chemical reaction: copper and related alloys rust into a grayish-green color due to prolonged exposure to damp air. This phenomenon can be seen on the copper covering of the Statue of Liberty!

076

AQUAMARINE

This term originated from the Latin "aqua marina," meaning seawater. Aquamarine is a fine stone from the beryl family and comes in the form of hexagonal crystals with a transparent, gentle blue color. This color is the product of iron molecules crystallizing. As early as the second century BC, Greeks and Romans believed aquamarine had the power to protect mariners from the wrath of the god of the sea... Poseidon.

077

GLACIAL MILK

What causes water to have a milky look about it when it tumbles down from the high mountains? When snow begins to melt, glacier water flows in torrents and acts like a grinder on the rocks. Fine mineral particles from the rocks, sometimes known as "rock flour," get into the water as it flows by. These tiny elements become suspended in the water and give it this beautiful shade of milky blue.

MINT DIABOLO

There is nothing quite like drinking a little mint diabolo to quench your thirst! Mint syrup added to lemonade produces a drink that, if made in the traditional way, has a color resembling green tea. Nowadays the syrup is no longer homemade, but is manufactured industrially — with artificial dyes! Mint diabolo is also called peppermint soda and to get its typical fresh hue, we mix the yellow E102 with the blue E131.

079

BLUE **SHELL**

Blue eggs? Surely, that cannot be possible... unless you're an American robin! During the mating season, the female robin lays a few delicately blue-hued eggs in her nest. This color is caused by a green bile pigment stored in her gallbladder that then dyes the egg during the laying process. This pigment is able to protect the egg from ultraviolet rays of the sun – just like a parasol!

080

TIFFANY® BLUE

Celebrated the world over, Tiffany & Co® is an American company selling luxury goods and jewelry. As early as 1878, it adopted a delicate, light blue color to adorn its jewelry boxes, bags and catalogs. This color may have been inspired by the mineral turquoise, which was a popular gemstone at the time. Established as an emblem, Tiffany® Blue contributed to the reputation of the brand, embodying both elegance and excellence.

081

CELESTE

When one mentions the color celeste in Italy, there is an urge to think about bicycles... At the end of the nineteenth century, this was the color adopted by the prestigious Italian manufacturer Bianchi® for its bikes and swimsuits. Celeste, the Italian sky blue, became a hit. According to legend, this shade was inspired by both the bright sky of Milan and the eyes of an Italian queen: Margherita of Savoy.

082

TURQUOISE

Turquoise is both a color and a fine stone. The stone has long been admired by many civilizations. Ancient Egyptians were mining it over 5,000 years ago! It can also be found on the other side of the world, where the Aztec peoples in Mexico used it to decorate several traditional objects. During the Middle Ages in Europe, it was called "Turkish stone" because Europeans imported it from Turkish merchants.

083

BLUE **LAGOON**

Deep in the middle of the ocean, a coral reef surrounds a body of water. This is a lagoon, yet why is it so blue? There are three reasons. Firstly, the blue of the sky is reflected on the water. Then there is the seabed, lined with a fine sand that radiates a light blue hue. Finally, there is the reef itself, which is home to a fragile ecosystem of phytoplankton that gives off a milky blue tint to these waters of paradise.

084

DUCK BLUE

This type of blue refers to the plumage of certain duck species, such as the mallard or teal. In mating seasons, iridescent blue feathers appear on the rear tips of the male duck's wings. These feathers can create a beautiful rainbow-like reflection that changes depending on the angle from which you see it. When winter returns, the male's plumage moults once more, showing a much more reserved color.

085

BLUE **FROG**

What in the world is the okopipi? This small, brightly colored tree frog is a true jewel of nature! However, we need to be very wary of it, as its color is a warning sign. The frog's skin conceals a poison capable of killing anything that tries to eat it. An Amazonian tribe used to coat the tips of their blowpipe darts with this paralyzing venom. That's why the frog is also known as the blue poison dart frog.

086

NAVY BLUE

Is there anyone who has never worn a sailor-style outfit with the white shirt and blue stripes? It's the classic image of the navy! The use of navy blue uniforms dates back to the eighteenth century. This rather gloomy shade was particularly suitable for the harsh conditions sailors had to face: it was highly resistant to sunlight and seawater. Some even thought it repelled rats and other vermin that stowed away on ships!

087

LAPIZ LAZULI

"Lapiz lazuli" comes from a Roman name meaning deep-blue stone. For over 7,000 years, this stone has been milled into a fine powder of intense blue. During the Renaissance, great masters like Raphael or Michelangelo used the powder for painting. Also known as ultramarine, this color was so expensive that it was only reserved for use on royal or divine figures.

WORK BLUE

During the nineteenth century, the Industrial Revolution gave birth to a number of factories where workers toiled over heavy machines on the production line. This is the century when blue working overalls appeared.

Dyed using the relatively inexpensive Prussian blue pigment, this standardized attire soon became symbolic of the whole working class.

089

ROYAL AIR FORCE

An important part of the British armed forces, the Royal Air Force is organized into fighter patrol and bomber groups that protect the United Kingdom from the air. Its greatest glory came during World War II, when British fighter pilots helped win the war for the Allies. Royal blue, on the other hand, stands for a mixture of shades close to azure blue — shades that resemble the sky on a clear day.

090

BLUE **JEANS**

The denim fabric for blue jeans was not actually invented in the USA, but in Italy! This very durable cotton textile was initially produced in Genoa. Exported throughout Europe and then to America, it became the work clothing of choice for lumberjacks and gold diggers during the age when the "West was won." Over time, blue jeans came to be a symbol of the American dream.

ICEBERG

An iceberg is a huge block of ice that floats freely in the sea. Icebergs are found near the coasts of Antarctica, Greenland and other frozen lands. Some are white and others a shade of blue. It all depends on their age. The older an iceberg is, the denser it becomes and the smoother and more reflective its surface is. Some are even striped like a zebra, exposing geological layers that go back thousands of years.

092

SKY BLUE

Bright blue seems to adorn the sky on a cloudless day. But this color is actually an optical illusion. When the sun's rays pierce through the atmosphere, they are sent in all directions by different molecules, each one appearing as either a violet or blue beam. Hence, we see the sky as a bluish color. Sky blue shades can vary depending on the position of the sun, the climate and the season of the year.

093

BLUE **HELMET**

The Blue Helmets are a military force organized by the United Nations. These troops come from a number of countries and are specifically assigned to protect civilians torn by local conflict. Stuck between two warring forces, Blue Helmets strive to maintain peace and international security. They can be distinguished from other soldiers by their sky blue headgear, which represents the color of their neutrality.

094

CHARETTE BLUE

In sixteenth-century southern France, there was a massive drive to cultivate a plant called "pastel," a raw material needed to produce the valuable pigment charette blue. Used by dyers to color fabrics, this pigment was also known to repel insects! Farmers therefore were known to mop up the bottoms of dyers' vats in order to acquire the material, which they later painted on their own equipment. Good bye, flies and mosquitoes!

095

CORNFLOWER BLUE

Why is the cornflower an emblem for French war veterans? Why did Britain choose the poppy to remember her fallen soldiers? Well, both of these flowers have something in common. They were both growing in the fields of countries ravaged by fighting during World War I. In France, the bleuet cornflower was chosen because it was also the name given to young soldiers as they went off to the battle in their blue uniforms.

096

TUAREG BLUE

The Tuaregs are nomadic herding people that live mainly in the Sahara Desert. Dressed in large blue shawls that protect them from the sun, sand and wind, they move about on the backs of camels. The fabrics of these shawls, which were traditionally dyed blue using indigo leaves, have the strange quality of coloring the Tuaregs' skin when they sweat. This is why they are called the "Blue People"!

097

BLUEBONNET

The bluebonnet is a variety of plant from the lupine family. Lupines have large blue flowers and are especially widespread throughout the wild prairies of Texas in the USA. They acquired the name "bluebonnet" after the headwear of pioneering women who helped settle Texas during the conquest of the American West. Bluebonnets are now the Texan state flower.

INDIGO

The word indigo comes from the Latin "indicum," which means Indian. This coloring material comes from the true indigo plant's leaves, which have been imported from India since the end of the seventeenth century.

Textile makers soaked their fabrics in vats containing juices from indigo leaves, which when exposed to air would oxidize and taint the fabric a deep blue.

099

MIDNIGHT BLUE

When night falls, the sun fades away and the sky darkens. Yet we don't perceive the true, deep black color of the universe at night. Instead, it appears to us as a dark blue. But why is this so? Is it an optical illusion?

Sources of light, such as airglow from the earth's atmosphere, prevent the night sky from looking completely black to us. Therefore, we recognize dark blue at nighttime.

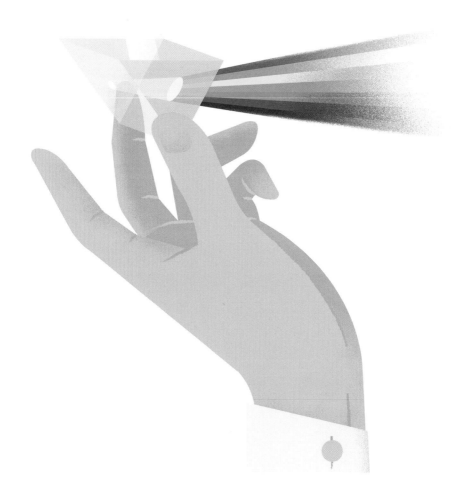

100

VIOLET

A color that is often mistaken as black, violet was even named "just black" in the Middle Ages. In the sixteenth century, violet was very much associated with sorrow and with deceased royalty who were enrobed in the color. Isaac Newton, the English scientist, contributed to violet's change of image. Watching the breakdown of colors through a prism, he named violet as the seventh category of the chromatic rainbow.

101

AMETHYST

This is a fine stone from the quartz family. Much used in jewelry making, amethysts have adorned precious items for centuries. The gemstone was believed to remedy the effects of alcohol, which explains its ancient Greek name "amethustos", meaning "without being drunk." Its violet tone and transparency resemble diluted wine. Amethysts consist partly of iron, and when they're heated they take on a lemony-yellow color.

102

PARMA VIOLET

In the eighteenth century, there was a delicate scent of violet in the air throughout the countryside near the city of Parma, Italy. This fragrant little flower was being grown and used to make a scented water much revered throughout Europe. French King Louis XIII used to cover himself with Parma talcum powder to disguise his own body odor!

PURPLE **BISHOP**

The color violet is particularly significant within the Catholic church. It's a prominent color on the outfits of bishops at certain times of the year, such as before Christmas and Easter. By wearing purple, the bishops demonstrate regrets for their sins and request the forgiveness of God. They complete their outfit with a violet amethyst stone on their right finger.

104

BRAZILWOOD

In the Middle Ages, exotic bresel wood was being imported to Europe by Venetian merchants returning from Asia. It was made into a precious pigment that could be used to dye fabrics in a variety of shades, from red to light purple. Around 1500, Portuguese sailors discovered a similar wood in South America. They gave it the name brazilwood... and they later christened the land where it was found as "Brazil."

105

MAUVE

In 1856, a young English chemist by the name of William Henry Perkin invented the first synthetic dye to be produced on an industrial scale. It became known as "mauveine" because its color resembled that of the mauve flower's petals. This coloring was used to treat fabrics such as wool or silk. Also worn by Queen Victoria, the British sovereign, the hue went on to become a resounding success in the world of fashion.

106

FUCHSIA

Fuchsia is another color that carries the name of a flower. This time it refers to a small shrub decorated by little blossoms. The plant was discovered on the Caribbean island of Hispaniola (now Haiti and the Dominican Republic) by Charles Plumier, a French botanist and explorer. As was customary at that time, Plumier named his plant after a person he admired: Leonhart Fuchs, the father of German botany.

107

MEXICAN PINK

What would a Mexican fiesta be without ponchos embroidered in Mexican pink? This color, popularized in the middle of the twentieth century, is a symbol of Mexican national identity. It's better known as the color magenta, which is an artificial dye used in textiles. Magenta dye also contains a compound that can be used for healing wounds.

BEET

The beet is a root vegetable that has been cultivated since ancient times. There are three varieties: white beets, best known for the production of white sugar; fodder beets, which are used to feed livestock; and the garden beets found on our dinner plates. A garden beet is distinguishable by its fleshy root and its purple hue, as well as its healthful properties as a food. It also contains the vegetable pigment betaine.

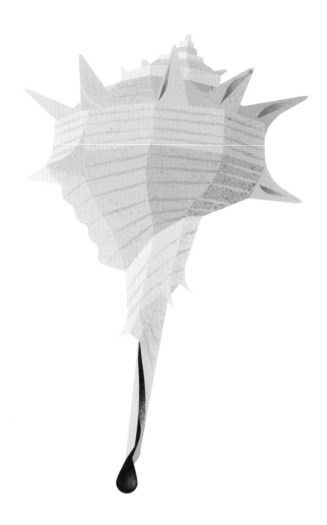

109

PURPLE

During antiquity, textiles dyed purple were counted among the most luxurious goods in the Mediterranean region. Much sought after and excessively expensive, this pigment was the result of a Murex sea snail secretion that had been marinated in urine. It took thousands of shell fish to create the precious pigment. The smell was so bad that the storage tanks were kept outside the city. Yikes, that's disgusting!

110

RED **FRUITS**

Redcurrant, strawberry, raspberry, cranberry, blueberry, cherry, blackberry, blackcurrant... What amazing flavors for our taste buds! The color of the flesh differs considerably from one fruit to the other. Yet they are all part of the same family of fruits. One thing they all have in common is that they contain anthocyanin. This is a vegetable pigment that enables the fruits to become blush red and to protect them against the sun's rays.

111

BLACK **BEETLE**

The dung beetle, also called the scarab beetle, is a particular variety of black beetle with the unusual habit of shaping balls of muck to feed its larvae (young). Through this behavior, it helps clean and fertilize the soil in which it lives — thus making up a key component of the whole ecosystem. At the time of the pharaohs in ancient Egypt, scarabs were regarded as sacred and as a symbol of renewal.

112

BLACK **INK**

For thousands of years, Chinese masters in the art of calligraphy have been producing marvelous drawings. Originally created from soot mixed with fish glue, this ink was applied to rice parchment with either a brush or reed stalk. In the West, goose feathers were used as "pens" to write manuscripts. The ink was created using iron sulphate and gallnut oil. To each his own!

PETROL BLUE

Petroleum comes from the Latin words "petra" for stone and "oleum" for oil. Often called simply "petrol," it's a natural mineral oil that has been buried deep underground for millennia. When in its raw state, this shiny substance is a deep black color. Yet when exposed to sunlight, it develops blue-green shades — hence the name petrol blue. Long a main source of energy, petroleum is becoming increasingly less obtainable.

114

PIRATE BLACK

Help, pirates are here! Identifiable by their flag (yes, the famous black one with the skull and crossbones), these sea bandits would do anything to capture a vessel they fancied. Before the attack, they would hoist their flag to encourage their enemy to surrender without a fight. If their opponents refused to back down, they would then replace the black flag with a red one, signaling a fight to the death. All aboard ship!

115

KOHL

Could you imagine Cleopatra without her famous eyeliner? With a grayish coloring material called kohl, she launched a fashion that would last from the days of ancient Egypt. In antiquity, kohl contained ground up lead and powdered antimony, which was thought to have the added virtue of protecting the eyes from various infections. All in all, it was a product made to delight the pharaohs!

ALL BLACKS

This is the nickname given to New Zealand's rugby football team. Highly regarded globally for its many championships, the team is renowned for its black oufits, similar to those of a pirate or rebel. It is also known for the Haka, a war dance accompanied by a Maori chant, which the players carry out just before every match to intimidate their opponents. "Ka mate! Ka mate! Ka ora! Ka ora!"

117

CHARCOAL BLACK

When ancient plants died, their remains became buried underground. Protected from the air for millions of years, they slowly degraded and were transformed into black charcoal. This substance was once a major source of energy — it was the first fossil fuel to be extracted from the ground. People used charcoal to warm their homes in the winter, operate their factories and, even today, produce electricity.

118

BLACK **PANTHER**

Lying in a dark and damp forest, a black panther lies in wait. This solitary cat is a member of the leopard family. If you look at a panther's coat very closely, you'll notice that it is slightly mottled with little flecks.

This feature is due to a condition called melanism, which increases the levels of dark skin pigment known as melanin. Black panthers use their special coloring for camouflage!

119

MUMMY BROWN

This pigment was once used by both painters and doctors. Apothecaries and pharmacists of earlier times sold it as a coloring agent or as a medication. However, they made sure to hide the secret of how the deep brown powder was created — namely by crushing down mummified bodies from Egypt and the East. You could say they kept the secret under wraps!

BROWN

The word "brown" in French was formerly used to describe anything dark or deep in color. Nowadays, it refers to a shade between chestnut and burnt brown. Often associated with soil and dead leaves, brown is especially widespread throughout nature. It can also be found on many animal species living in forested areas, such as the brown bear, the wild boar and the roe deer. Quite a handy color for hiding in the woods!

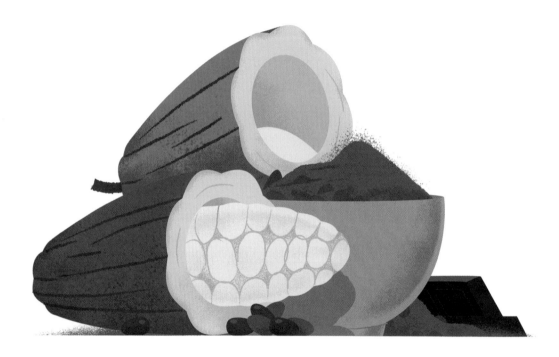

121

COCOA

What is the recipe for cocoa? It all starts with cocoa beans. These grains are harvested, then fermented and roasted at a temperature of 320 degrees Fahrenheit (160 degrees Celsius), which releases their aromas and gives the bean its chracteristic brown color. Finally, they are ground down into cocoa powder, which is essential for the production of delicious, deep brown hot chocolate. Yum!

122

POOP

Cow or elephant dung, horse manure, goat muck, bird droppings, deer filth, wild boar excrement, otter feces: these are all terms used to describe excrement or, more familiarly, "poop." The general color of poop is deep brown. But as a rule, its consistency, smell, shape and color will vary depending on the diet of the individual animal. That's for sure!

LICORICE

At one time or another, we have all tasted these strange black sweets. But where does their distinct taste come from? Nicknamed "soft wood," licorice comes from a shrub whose aromatic roots have been harvested since ancient times. You only need to chew the bark to extract the juice and perfume. As well as being deliciously sweet, licorice also has medicinal properties. So, why deprive yourself? Try some!

124

GRAPHITE

What do all these things have in common: a mechanical pencil, a plumb line and a wooden pencil? It's graphite! First discovered in England at the end of the seventeenth century, graphite has become an essential component of the pencil – a tool first devised by French inventor Nicolas Jacques Conté. "Plumb lines" go back to Roman times, when a tip of base metal was used in surveying, or measuring out plots of land.

125

BASALT GRAY

When molten magma spews out of a volcano, it is in liquid form and fiery red in color. Its hue however will always depend on its current temperature, so at 1,650 degrees Fahrenheit (900 degrees Celsius) it is dark red, but above 2,100 °F (1,150 °C) it turns yellow. On cooling, it hardens into a dark gray rock: basalt. Huge columns of basalt can be seen at a famous natural landmark in Northern Ireland called "The Giant's Causeway"!

126

CHARTREUSE BLUE

At one time, the Chartreux cat was greatly prized for its thick gray-blue coat, which was used to make soft and silky fabrics. But where does the cat's name come from? Legend has it that hermit monks sheltered the animals at the foot of the Chartreuse mountain range in France, in order to fight off rats and other pests. Thanks to them, therefore, all the manuscripts and food supplies were spared.

127

BLUE **WHALE**

The blue whale is the largest animal in the world. It can sometimes reach over 170 tons in weight and 100 feet (30 meters) in length. With its colossal appetite, it can consume over 4 tons of small krill (tiny shrimp) daily.

On the surface, its body is an almost gray slate color. Yet when it dives in the deep, the whale takes on a bluish shimmer. This is because its speckled pigmentation absorbs the blue tones of the water.

128

MOUNTBATTEN PINK

This mixed pink and gray tone is said to have been invented during World War II by the British admiral Louis Mountbatten. According to his theory, the color would enable ships to blend into the background. Experience, however, did not prove Mountbatten's claim to be so convincing; and after a few months, English ships reverted to a more effective coating for disguise.

PEBBLE GRAY

Slate, granite, quartz, ... Every pebble found on a beach is a fragment of rock. After being tossed about by waves on the sea shore or by river currents, the rocks become eroded and take on a smooth, rounded shape. Their colors vary depending on the rock from which they originated. Yet when you look at them from a distance, their general appearance is, by and large, that of a grayish shade. It's a neat optical illusion!

130

ASH WHITE

Plants draw trace elements and essential minerals from the sun that they need to grow. When plants are burned, they change first into a glowing red ember, then a black charcoal and finally to ash — which can be red, yellow or white. Ash color will always depend on the amount of minerals that were initially contained in the plant and the surrounding earth. The richer in calcium the plant had been, the whiter its ash will be!

131

APHRODITE'S TEARS

Mother of pearl (or nacre) is a rare, sought after object that was highly prized in ancient times. It's sometimes called "tears of Aphrodite," after the Greek goddess of beauty. But where does it come from? When an impurity enters the shell of an oyster or other mollusk, the animal envelops it with limestone. Mother of pearl generally has a clear gray color, with a glimmer of pink and blue.

132

FLOWER OF SALT

Salt has been collected since prehistoric times, from the salt marshes off the Mediterranean coast to the Atlantic Ocean. Seawater that is trapped in shallow basins evaporates and leaves behind salt residue.

Flower of salt is one of the finest salts on Earth. On first being harvested, it appears to be a pinky-gray. However, it is not dirty — there are minerals in the salt that provide it with that appearance.

133

MOONLIGHT

The whiteness of the moon illuminates the deep dark of the night. However, it does not emit light. Its surface is covered with particles of gray dust that reflect the light from the sun, just like tiny marbles. So, when the moon is at its zenith, we perceive it to be extremely white. Its color, however, will differ depending on its position in the atmosphere. In our eyes, it is never the same.

ANNEXES

COLOR PALETTE

001	WHITE SNOW	032	RED CARD
002	MILK	033	ENGLISH RED
003	PEACE SYMBOL	034	INDIAN SUMMER
004	ALBINOS	035	MARS RED
005	ALABASTER	036	CLAY
006	POLAR WHITE	037	SAFFRON
007	COTTON FLOWER	038	ORANGE
008	BIRCH BARK	039	CARROT
009	WHITE MOTH	040	CARROT TOP
010	WHITE POWDER	041	FAWN
011	MARSHMALLOWS	042	AMBER
012	COTTON CANDY	043	CAMEL HAIR
013	PINK PIGGY	044	OCHRE
014	BABY PINK	045	KHAKI
015	ROSE	046	OFF-WHITE
016	CHERRY BLOSSOM	047	BEIGE
017	PINK	048	EGG SHELL
018	PINK SHRIMP	049	DESERT ROSE
019	PINK FLAMINGO	050	SEPIA
020	RISING SUN	051	TURMERIC
021	POMME GRENADE	052	INDIAN YELLOW
022	RED KISSES	053	CATERPILLAR®
023	CANNONBALL RED	054	BIC®
024	RUBY	055	EGG YOLK
025	OXBLOOD	056	SECURITY YELLOW
026	RED PENNSY	057	SUNFLOWER
027	CARMINE	058	POLLEN
028	CARDINAL RED	059	CANARY YELLOW
029	POPPY	060	IVORY
030	ROOSTER	061	FLOWERS OF SULPHUR
031	FERRARI® RED	062	GLOWWORM

063	KIWI GREEN
064	BEDBUG
065	GREEN WITH ANGER
066	CHLOROPHYLL
067	BOTTLE GREEN
068	BRITISH GREEN
069	CEDAR BLUE
070	LINCOLN GREEN
071	ARSENIC
072	GLAUCOUS
073	LICHEN
074	CELADON
075	VERDIGRIS
076	AQUAMARINE
077	GLACIAL MILK
078	MINT DIABOLO
079	BLUE SHELL
080	TIFFANY® BLUE
081	CELESTE
082	TURQUOISE
083	BLUE LAGOON
084	DUCK BLUE
085	BLUE FROG
086	NAVY BLUE
087	LAPIZ LAZULI
088	WORK BLUE
089	ROYAL AIR FORCE
090	BLUE JEANS
091	ICEBERG
092	SKY BLUE
093	BLUE HELMET
094	CHARETTE BLUE
095	CORNFLOWER BLUE
096	TUAREG BLUE
097	BLUEBONNET
098	INDIGO

099	MIDNIGHT BLUE
100	VIOLET
101	AMETHYST
102	PARMA VIOLET
103	PURPLE BISHOP
104	BRAZILWOOD
105	MAUVE
106	FUCHSIA
107	MEXICAN PINK
108	BEET
109	PURPLE
110	RED FRUITS
111	BLACK BEETLE
112	BLACK INK
113	PETROL BLUE
114	PIRATE BLACK
115	KOHL
116	ALL BLACKS
117	CHARCOAL BLACK
118	BLACK PANTHER
119	MUMMY BROWN
120	BROWN
121	COCOA
122	POOP
123	LICORICE
124	GRAPHITE
125	BASALT GRAY
126	CHARTREUSE BLUE
127	BLUE WHALE
128	MOUNTBATTEN PINK
129	PEBBLE GRAY
130	ASH WHITE
131	APHRODITE'S TEARS
132	FLOWER OF SALT
133	MOONLIGHT

THEMATIC INDEX

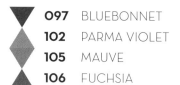

097 BLUEBONNET
102 PARMA VIOLET
105 MAUVE
106 FUCHSIA

108 BEET
110 RED FRUITS

TREES

008 BIRCH BARK
016 CHERRY BLOSSOM
034 INDIAN SUMMER
042 AMBER
066 CHLOROPHYLL
069 CEDAR BLUE
104 BRAZILWOOD

SWEET DELICACIES

011 MARSHMALLOWS
012 COTTON CANDY
078 MINT DIABOLO
121 COCOA
123 LICORICE

OTHER PLANTS & ORGANISMS

011 MARSHMALLOWS
051 TURMERIC
066 CHLOROPHYLL
072 GLAUCOUS
073 LICHEN
094 CHARETTE BLUE
098 INDIGO
123 LICORICE
130 ASH WHITE

CLOTHES & FABRICS

014 BABY PINK
027 CARMINE
043 CAMEL HAIR
046 OFF-WHITE
047 BEIGE
052 INDIAN YELLOW
090 BLUE JEANS
097 BLUEBONNET
098 INDIGO
104 BRAZILWOOD
105 MAUVE
107 MEXICAN PINK
109 PURPLE

FRUITS & VEGETABLES

021 POMME GRENADE
038 ORANGE
039 CARROT
063 KIWI GREEN

OFFICIAL OUTFITS

028 CARDINAL RED
070 LINCOLN GREEN
088 WORK BLUE
096 TUAREG BLUE

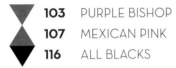

◆

Whilst
investi-
gating the
world of colors,
shades and tones, you
may find that you lose
your way. Throughout my
work on this book, my main ob-
jective was to gather as much
knowledge as I could. Key to this was
learning about the array of contrasts between
the colors. I was equally guided by my childhood memories and by my experience in practice and
from the art academy. Above all, researching this
huge subject matter stretched my professional capabilities
to their limit. I was able to collate all kinds of technical,
scientific, historical, etymological and linguistic information that
lent a playful and poetic dimension to the book. Naturally, I was
also influenced by my own personal fascination for colors and their
subtle shades. The following list outlines the main stages of my journey. My
starting point involved books by Annie Mollard-Desfour and Michel Pastoureau.
The works by Annie Mollard-Desfour are (all titles from Éditions C.N.R.S.): Le Rose
(2002), Le Blanc (2008), Le Rouge (2009), Le Noir (2010), Le Vert (2012), Le Bleu (2013) and Le
Gris (2015). Books by Michel Pastoureau and Dominique Simonnet are (all titles by Éditions du
Seuil, some from the series 'Points'): Le Petit Livre des couleurs; Michel Pastoureau, Vert, histoire
d'une couleur (2013); Bleu, histoire d'une couleur (2014); Noir, histoire d'une couleur (2014); Les Couleurs
de nos souvenirs (2015); Rouge, histoire d'une couleur (2016). Delving further, I also leaned on a few
specialist publications: Eugène Chevreul, Moyen de nommer et de définir les couleurs, Mémoires de l'Aca-
démie des sciences de l'Institut de France, Paris, 1861; Maurice Déribéré, La Couleur, Paris, P.U.F., Reihe
"Que sais-je ?" (1964); François Delamare und Bernard Guineau, Les Matériaux de la couleur, Paris,
Éditions Gallimard, Reihe "Découvertes" (1999); Philippe Nessmann, Un monde en couleurs, Paris,
Éditions Gallimard Jeunesse (2011). Additionally, a few answers to my many questions
were provided by two leading course books: Roches et minéraux, Paris, Éditions Gallimard Jeunesse, Reihe "Les Thématiques de l'encyclopédi@" (2005) and Encyclopédie
des animaux, Paris, Éditions Gallimard Jeunesse, Reihe "Les Yeux de la découverte"
(2013). One dictionary and two encyclopedias helped me very much in ve-
rifying quite a lot of information: Le Petit Larousse, Encyclopédie Larousse
and Encyclopédie Universalis. Newspapers, magazines and several
articles also provided me with the opportunity to unearth
untold treasures and to pep up my research activities:
Science & vie, Ça m'intéresse, The Huffington Post, Le
Monde, Futura sciences, Le Nouvel Obs, Sciences et
avenir, La Croix, Le Figaro and Le Parisien. Ultimately, countless color charts accompanied
me on my journey. These materials
proved to be both an important
reference source as well as
an inspiration: ColorHexa,
Pourpre.com, Encycolor-
pédia, Dulux Valen-
tine, RAL, Farrow
& Ball and
Pantone.

◆

Many thanks to Gaston, who with his six years took over the role of the small artistic director. To Véronique, for her patience, her support and commitment. To Simon, who has been with me on my paint expeditions for several years. And, finally, to all others who have assisted in the making of this work from near or far...

♦

Originally published by Editions Gallimard Jeunesse under the title COLORAMA. Imagier des nuances de couleurs
© Editions Gallimard Jeunesse, 2017
© for the illustrations, texts and typography: Cruschiform, 2017
© for the English edition:
Prestel Verlag, 2017, Munich · London · New York
A member of Verlagsgruppe Random House GmbH
Neumarkter Straße 28 · 81673 Munich

Prestel Publishing Ltd.
14-17 Wells Street
London W1T 3PD

Prestel Publishing
900 Broadway, Suite 603
New York, NY 10003

Library of Congress Control Number: 2017943312
A CIP catalogue record for this book is available from the British Library.

Translation from French by Paul Kelly
Copyediting: Brad Finger
Editorial direction: Doris Kutschbach
Project management: Melanie Schöni
Production management: Corinna Pickart
Paper: Amber Graphic

Verlagsgruppe Random House FSC® N001967
Printed in Italy

ISBN 978-3-7913-7328-7

www.prestel.com